ON
FORGIVENESS

'I wish that more writers commanded Holloway's ability to write a small book about big ideas . . . His excellence as a spiritual *agent provocateur* lies in sticking to the essentials of his argument'
The Times

'Anyone who has ever dealt with him, knows him to be the kindest of men and he has written an important book'
Scotsman

'Lively, thought-provoking, elegantly expressed . . . it casts light on a problematic – and increasingly critical – subject'
Herald

'I don't know when I have been more impressed, indeed, excited, by a work . . . It answers the seemingly unanswerable tormenting questions in a completely satisfying way'   Ruth Rendell

'A work of blinding sincerity and high intelligence'   *Spectator*

'Confirms Richard Holloway's place as our most thoughtful religious revisionist and secular moralist'   *Sunday Herald*

'His liberal apostasy over matters of gay relationships and morality without God has made him a hate figure for some traditionalists, but this book should win them round. Written in an engaging and easy wa[y] . . . [dist]inctive Christian vi[sion] . . . *Times*

Also by Richard Holloway

ON
FORGIVENESS

RICHARD HOLLOWAY

CANONGATE
Edinburgh · London

This Canons edition published in 2015
by Canongate Books

First published in Great Britain in 2002 by
Canongate Books Ltd, 14 High Street,
Edinburgh EH1 1TE

www.canongate.tv

1

British Library Cataloguing-in-Publication Data
A catalogue record for this book is available on
request from the British Library

ISBN 978 1 78211 628 8

Printed and bound in Great Britain by Clays Ltd, St Ives plc

For Desmond Tutu

There is only forgiveness, if there is any,
where there is the unforgivable.

Jacques Derrida

Contents

He hath shewed thee, O man, what is good;
and what doth the Lord require of thee, but
to do justly, and to love mercy, and to walk
humbly with thy God.

From the Hebrew Scriptures

Ye have heard that it hath been said, Thou
shalt love thy neighbour, and hate thine
enemy. But I say unto you, Love your
enemies, bless them that curse you, do
good to them that hate you, and pray
for them which despitefully use you,
and persecute you.

From the Christian Scriptures

Repair the evil done to you with
something that is better. And lo!
The enemy who did evil to you may
turn into a close and true friend.

From the Moslem Scriptures

Introduction

One of the unexpected and enriching things about writing books is watching the life they have after they are published and leave the author's control. I am not talking about the praise or blame, enthusiasm or hostility of critics and reviewers. I am thinking about the separate existence books achieve in the lives of readers and the responses they provoke. Over the years since it was published, this book has brought me, however fleetingly, alongside people at difficult moments in their lives. And what intrigued me was that they responded to the book not so much as a thesis they agreed or disagreed with, but as a question that prompted a reply. It was obvious from what they told me that the refusal to forgive could be as freeing for some as the decision to forgive was liberating for others. Writing the book was never a theoretical exercise for me, but the response to it reminded me – if I needed reminding – that the problem of forgiveness is a raw, existential reality for many people.

There was the wife from the shelter for abused women

who told me that it was her capacity to go on forgiving her abusive husband that nearly got her killed; while it was her anger and desire for justice that released her from his cruelty and gave her and her children a better life.

There was the mother whose daughter was murdered who, because she was a Christian who found herself unable to forgive her child's killer, withdrew from membership of the Church.

There was the man who had been sexually abused by his parish priest as a child whose adult life was now consumed in pursuing his abuser and the Church that had protected him.

While fully understanding these responses and the anger that energised them, I was intrigued that they had felt it necessary to tell me about them. The implication seemed to be that my book had sought to impose an obligation on people to forgive in all circumstances, whereas that was the opposite of what I had intended. It was because I was very aware of the damaging effect pressure to forgive could have on people who found it impossible that I had been careful to describe my book as descriptive not prescriptive, as written not in the imperative but in the indicative mood. I was trying to say: look, human beings do terrible things to each other and the tragic thing about it all is the way the remembrance of past hurt can rob us of our future and become the narrative of our lives, like Coleridge's Ancient Mariner whose only release comes from rehearsing the tragedy that had consumed him. One can recognise the pain in these trapped lives without condemnation or disapproval, or even praying that an easier way could open for them. Nietzsche, brilliant psychologist that he was, was well aware of this phenomenon, and in a passage I quoted reminded us how people differed in their ability to prevent incidents from the past becoming the gravediggers of the present.

I had noticed this difference myself in a lifetime of pastoral encounters with people. Some seemed to have an infinite capacity for forgiveness, others hardly any. Some were able to recover quickly from great wrongs done to them; others were devastated by a single slight. Nietzsche said we had to know something of the 'plastic energy' of a person if we would account for the way they respond to life's blows. That's why to know all would be to forgive all, including the inability to forgive. And it was why I had spent some time in my book trying to uncover the way we are all determined by factors that were never in our control; suggesting that we only get leverage on our weaknesses when we begin to acknowledge and accept their existence.

So I was well aware of the danger of trying to force people to feel they had to forgive when it was impossible or even morally destructive for them to do so.

But the fact remained that forgiveness, however we account for its absence or presence in ourselves or in others, has an almost mystical capacity for healing the hurts of the past and restoring the future. And part of the mystery of its working is that it can sometimes operate without apparent human volition. Another mother who was in touch with me told me she had insisted on meeting the gaoled killer of her daughter in order to challenge him with what he had done, and found herself suddenly and spontaneously forgiving him; to which he immediately responded with a tearful confession of his guilt. I had taken the epigram for my book from Jacques Derrida: *There is only forgiveness, if there is any, where there is the unforgivable*, and this had struck me as a stunning example of that paradox.

So what is this mysterious force in human relationships that can heal wounds and mend shattered relationships not only between individuals but between groups and sometimes even between nations? In this book I never tried to venture a definition by which it could be understood or to offer a process by which it could be achieved. What I found myself doing was circling round the mystery of it all, though here and there I tried to point to its most telling characteristics. It was clearly important to make a distinction between forgiving the person and forgiving the act. A terrible act must never be forgiven or we lose our ability to discern between right and wrong, good and evil. But the *agent* of a terrible act may have to be forgiven if we are ever to free ourselves from its consequences and reclaim the future it has stolen from us.

Sometimes the mechanics of forgiveness are simple and conditional: we say we are sorry, we acknowledge the harm we have done; those we trampled upon regain their dignity and reconciliation is won. Hard enough between individuals, this kind of reconciliation is even harder between communities, but when it is achieved bridges can be thrown over chasms and deserts can blossom again like the rose.

Conditional forgiveness may be hard to do, but it is easy to understand how it works. It is a transaction we all have to negotiate if we want to sustain the relationships in which our lives are enfolded, which is why there is always a sense in which the metrics of the market place apply to it: we bargain with each other to keep the system going because we are all invested in its benefits. But when we come to Derrida's forgiveness of the unforgiveable all bets are off, all transactions voided: and we are faced with what theologians call pure grace. It is gift with no thought of return; a miracle of generosity for its own sake. And there seems to be an unpremeditated helplessness about it, best captured in the Parable of the Prodigal Son – which I talk about in the last chapter – in which the father's heart breaks at the sight of his broken son stumbling up the hill towards him.

Like Jacques Derrida, who thanked me for the book when it came out, I saw this uncalculating grace at work in Desmond Tutu and Nelson Mandela when South

Africa emerged from the long nightmare of apartheid. I dedicated the book to Desmond Tutu, and when it came out he wrote to thank me and told me he found the ending 'quite devastating' and that it had left him 'shattered'.

Maybe that's because the book ends with a warning that societies which are unable to forgive the past are destined always to repeat it.

Richard Holloway

CHAPTER ONE

Religion without Religion

You don't have to be religious to believe in or practise forgiveness. You might even argue that religion can make people invincibly unforgiving, but the fact remains that religion gives us many of the best stories and metaphors for forgiveness. The difficulty we face in using these texts is in defining the authority of the language they come in. It is proclaiming the obvious to say that words mean different things to different people. Because we tend to operate on the assumption that *our* words have some sort of equivalence to the things they describe, we are always surprised when they puzzle or confuse other people rather than enlighten them. This is not only over the obvious difficulty of using another language incompetently: even the language we know best contains traps for the unwary. One of the enduringly comic situations afforded by life is the studied incomprehension of the previous generation when it stumbles on the new meaning that words have been given by the next generation. We might, for example, hear an elderly gentleman mourning the appropriation of the word *gay* by the homosexual community. I remember watching a perplexed presenter on a television panel game trying to get her head round the black slang of one of her contestants who was insisting that *wicked* was a word of high praise. Part of our genius as humans is the way we go on adapting language to fit our changing experience of life and the mysterious universe in which it is set.

However, this task of adaptation is problematic when we try to apply it to the sacred texts of religion. That is why in this introductory chapter I want to explain my approach to the big words that religion deals in and the ideas that lie behind them, such as forgiveness, the principal topic of this book. First of all, I want to say that I shall try very hard to be descriptive rather than prescriptive in what I write. This is not what people usually expect from religious writing. Religion is associated in their minds with the imperative mood, with rules and commandments that allegedly come directly from God and must therefore be obeyed without question. I do not want to retrace ground I have already covered in a previous book, *Godless Morality*, except to repeat the point that to identify God with social arrangements that come from a previous stage of human development makes any kind of cultural evolution impossible. Traditional religions claim that God has provided a highly detailed and permanent pattern for human relationships, and the fact that it happens to be based on the cultural norms of ancient patriarchal societies is just too bad; ours is not to reason why. Universal obedience to this claim would have put a permanent brake on cultural development, had religion been the only player in the game. Fortunately, the evolution of the secular mind has increasingly limited the power of religion to inhibit the pace of social change, so that the current of human liberation has been able to flow largely unimpeded. The movement of ideas in eighteenth-century Europe that became known as the Enlightenment began to undermine the role of religious authority as the main determinant of human values. The religions themselves were increasingly discredited by their conflicts and rivalries, so the secular mind gradually won the battle for tolerance against its divided enemy. It is beyond dispute that the victory of secular humanism has created a major crisis for Christianity. The Church was in a position of cultural dominance in the West for centuries. It saw itself not as one religion among many, but as the final and complete way appointed by God for humans to achieve salvation. It is difficult for a religion accustomed to think of itself as the only true way of life to adapt to a pluralist culture where its claims are tolerated as only one choice among many. It is also well known that when institutions that were founded to propagate great ideas are threatened by the revolutions of history they tend to protect themselves by retreating behind their own walls, at the expense of the values they were designed to promote. Their own survival then becomes their main purpose, rather than the promotion of their best ideals.

The counterpoint to the current panic in institutional religion is the arrogance of the purely secular mind that refuses to acknowledge that religion has been the main carrier of certain fundamental values. I shall argue in this book that religion has been the container of some important human discoveries that are still vital to us, even though the institutions that carried them through time may be disintegrating. That is why I want to be descriptive rather than prescriptive in what I write. I want to argue that an exploration of forgiveness, a description of how it works and where it comes from, will enrich our humanity, whether or not we continue to hold specifically religious beliefs.

When I take part in radio discussions on religion, I am frequently challenged by people to give a straight yes or no in answer to their questions about the meaning of particular passages in the Bible. I always resist these attempts to turn theology into algebra, by pointing out that there are honestly different ways of using and understanding religious narratives. What is important is to use them to improve rather than damage the health of the human community. We are more likely to agree on that objective than on establishing their precise theological meaning. This way of using religion tries to show that some of its best values are now accepted by the community at large, so the important thing is to concentrate on the continuing development of these values and pay less attention to the agencies that have carried them through history. Like the rocket that has to fall away when it has established its satellite in space, religion has thrust its best values into the human orbit where we hope they will continue to do their work long after the vehicle that got them there has disappeared. What happens to the launch engine is not as important as the future of the ideals it has carried, though there will be some sadness as we see it disintegrating now that its purpose has been achieved. This approach continues to accord a high value to the impulse behind *religion*, though it no longer takes any of the particular *religions* at their own self-estimation. It is a position that Jacques Derrida calls 'religion without religion'. According to this way of looking at things, it is the fundamental ideals we find in religions that matter, not the religions themselves. The most important of these ideals, the love of God, has been the most difficult to define. This is how John Caputo puts it, as he echoes the famous question of Augustine of Hippo from his Confessions:

> What do I love when I love my God? Not the burnt offerings and solemn assemblies, but justice. Is justice then another name for God? Or is God another name for justice? If I serve the neighbour in the name of God, or if I serve the neighbour in the name of justice, what difference does it make? If the name of God is a *how*, not a *what*, then the name of God is *effective* even when it is not used.[1]

Caputo's emphasis on justice is interesting, because justice is one of the fundamental principles of the three religions that stem from Abraham: Judaism, Christianity and Islam. The call of justice is one aspect of faith that can continue to challenge us, even if we have abandoned the religious claim on which it is based. Indeed, one way of getting the present war on terrorism into some kind of perspective is to acknowledge the strong sense among Moslems that the West has been unjust in its handling of some of the conflicts in the Arab world. If justice is one of the fundamental principles of true religion, then forgiveness, as I shall argue, is its essential counterpart, its necessary antithesis. If our passion for justice can sometimes trap us in war and bitterness, then it is forgiveness that can sometimes help to rescue us. And, as with justice, we can value forgiveness for its own sake, even if we are no longer comfortable with the theological packaging it comes in. Indeed, we might argue that practising justice and forgiveness for their own sake, and not out of religious duty, is their highest expression and the truest form of religion. This is why Caputo goes on to say that the idea of religion without religion

> amounts to the recommendation that we return to the medieval sense of *vera religio*, where 'religion' meant a virtue, not a body with institutional headquarters in Nashville or the Vatican, so 'true religion' meant the 'virtue' of being genuinely or truly religious, of genuinely or truly loving God, not The One True Religion, Ours-versus-yours. God is more important than religion, as the ocean is more important than the raft, the latter bearing all the marks of being constituted by human beings. Religion, which is a human practice, is always deconstructible in the light of the love of God, which is not deconstructible.[2]

This way of applying some of the fundamental ideals of religion to the needs of the human community could help to lead us out of old conflicts into a new future. The fascinating thing about this radical hope in the possibilities of the future is the way some of its central protagonists, such as Hannah Arendt, Jacques Derrida and John Caputo, have developed a theory of human development that is continuous with the best of the religious vision. Though they do not accept the absolutist claims that religions have made for themselves, they affirm and admire the essence of the religious impulse, because it has promoted some of the best ideals of humanity. This is why Derrida uses the paradoxical formula, 'religion without religion'. Most people of common sense have long since intuited their way to a similar position, though they would express it in simpler language. Instinctively, they are repelled by the arrogant claims that certain religions make about possessing unique and exclusive versions of the truth without which the rest of us cannot be saved. They admire the way religions at their best produce people who are benefactors of humanity, servants of the poor, supporters and champions of the weak. While they may no longer practise religion seriously themselves, they like the way it continues to challenge human folly and cruelty. I am going to use the term *reconstructionist* to describe this revisionist approach to religion, and I want to apply it to the important theme of forgiveness in what follows in this book. And since I believe that the real meaning of religion is in deed not word, is a *how* not a *what*, I can be united in action with my more traditional sisters and brothers, even though our attitudes to the claims of theology may be very different.

A good example of how the reconstructionist approach to religion can confront our moral indifference is provided by the philosopher Richard Rorty. Rorty describes himself as an atheist, but he continues to place what I would call religious challenges before the human community. In his generous essay *Failed Prophecies, Glorious Hopes*, he describes how the utopian prophecies of both the New Testament and Karl Marx's *Communist Manifesto* have been repeatedly falsified by history, yet continue to represent the unconquerable human hope for justice and peace on earth. He points out that the eighteenth and nineteenth centuries witnessed a shift in the direction of human hope from eternity to our time on earth, from the longing for divine intervention to practical planning for the happiness of future generations. Rorty wishes we had documents that lacked the defects of the New Testament and the Manifesto, but he writes:

> It would be best, in short, if we could get along without prophecy and claims to knowledge of the

forces which determine history – if generous hope could sustain itself without such reassurances. Some day perhaps we shall have a new text to give our children – one which abstains from prediction yet still expresses the same yearning for fraternity as does the New Testament, and is as filled with sharp-eyed description of our most recent forms of inhumanity to each other as the Manifesto. But in the meantime we should be grateful for two texts which have helped make us better – have helped us overcome, to some degree, our brutish selfishness and our cultivated sadism.[3]

I shall make more use of the work of Jacques Derrida in this book than that of Richard Rorty, but I believe that both are talking about a process of Christianising the world without any necessary reference to the Church as such. In his short but powerful essay *On Cosmopolitanism and Forgiveness*, Derrida, in writing about the work of the Truth and Reconciliation Committee in South Africa, discusses the relatively new concept of a 'crime against humanity':

> . . . if, as I believe, the concept of a crime against humanity is the main charge of this self-accusation, of this repenting and this asking forgiveness; if, on the other hand, only a sacredness of the human can, in the

last resort, justify this concept; if this sacredness finds its meaning in the Abrahamic memory of the religions of the Book, and in a Jewish but above all Christian interpretation of the 'neighbour' or the 'fellow man'; if, from this, the crime against humanity is a crime against what is most sacred in the living, and thus already against the divine in man, in God-made-man or man-made-God-by-God, then the 'globalisation' of forgiveness resembles an immense scene of confession in progress, thus a virtually Christian convulsion-conversion-confession, a process of Christianisation which has no more need for the Christian church.[4]

And a few pages later he writes:

In order to approach now the very concept of forgiveness, logic and common sense agree for once with the paradox: it is necessary, it seems to me, to begin with the fact that, yes, there is the unforgivable. Is this not, in truth, the only thing to forgive? The only thing that calls for forgiveness? One cannot, or should not, forgive; there is only forgiveness, if there is any, where there is the unforgivable.[5]

I have used those extraordinary words as an epigraph to this book and I shall try to demonstrate that, in our day, perhaps for the first time since Jesus, forgiveness can be explored in all its profound but redemptive impossibility as a fundamental theme in human history. Though I shall refer to some Christian texts, particularly to the great parable of the Prodigal Son, I shall offer a reading that, while not denying the theological authority of the narratives, is mainly interested in their human meaning and application, in what Derrida calls 'religion without religion' or a process of Christianisation that has no more need of the Christian Church. The thing that attracts me to this approach is that it runs counter to what has always been the worst aspect of religion, which is its tendency to divide people from one another in both time and eternity. The method I shall use could unite us all, because it takes the great religious themes of hope and forgiveness and tries to make them work for the whole human community. I shall be more interested in discovering what forgiveness is and how it actually operates in the human sphere than in trying to promote or justify it. It makes no sense to command people to forgive, and there are clearly situations where every instinct of justice commands us not to forgive. Nevertheless, when true forgiveness happens it is one of the most astonishing and liberating of the human experiences. The tragedy of the many ways we trespass upon each other is that we can damage people so deeply that we rob them of the future by stopping the movement of their lives at the moment of the injury, which continues to send out shock-waves of pain that swamp their whole existence. I have called the next chapter, 'Reclaiming the Future', because forgiveness, when it happens, is able to remove that dead weight from our past and give us back our lives. The real beauty and power of forgiveness is that it can deliver the future to us.

CHAPTER TWO

Reclaiming the Future

At the end of the previous chapter I quoted from Jacques Derrida: 'There is only forgiveness, if there is any, where there is the unforgivable.' How did we get from the moment of creation to the point where human beings might even find it possible to forgive the unforgivable? My intention in the rest of this book is to attempt an answer to that question. And I want to start with a paragraph I scribbled into my note book over thirty years ago. It came from a Jewish American journalist called Harry Golden.

I have a rule against registering complaints in a restaurant; because I know that there are at least four billion suns in the Milky Way – which is only one galaxy. Many of these suns are thousands of times larger than our own, and vast millions of them have whole planetary systems, including literally billions of satellites, and all of this revolves at the rate of about a million miles an hour, like a huge oval pinwheel. Our own sun and its planets, which includes the earth, are on the edge of this wheel. This is only our small corner of the universe, so why do not these billions of revolving and rotating suns and planets collide? The answer is, the space is so unbelievably vast that if we reduced the suns and the planets in correct mathematical proportion with relation to the distances between them, each sun would be a speck of dust, two, three and four thousand miles away from its nearest neighbour. And, mind you, this is only the Milky Way – our own small corner – our own galaxy. How many galaxies are there? Billions. Billions of galaxies spaced at about one million light-years apart (one light-year is about six trillion miles). Within the range of our biggest telescopes there are at least one hundred million separate galaxies such as our own Milky Way, and that is not all, by any means. The scientists have found that the further you go out into space with the telescopes the thicker the galaxies become, and there are billions of billions as yet uncovered to the scientist's camera and astrophysicist's calculations.

When you think of all this, it's silly to worry whether the waitress brought you string beans instead of limas.[1]

In that quotation from a book published in 1959, Harry Golden's take on the science of the universe might be a bit dated, but I hope the point being made is clear: our private human concerns appear to be dwarfed and made meaningless by the immensity of the universe. However, even if at first we accept that judgment, a powerful and creative paradox begins to emerge. It is the gift of Harry Golden's consciousness that enabled him to set his dietary preferences in proportion to the scale of the universe, but that very act of comparison is itself an astounding fact. Insensate immensity, of itself, is of little value; but the fact that through us the universe is now aware of its own vastness and complexity begins to make the whole weird business of life much more interesting. According to the current scientific narrative, the universe was born in a violent shock that physicists call the Big Bang. However we account for its origins, it is a story of power exploding through expanding space. When I first wrote that sentence I talked about the universe expanding through space, then I got a letter from someone who had heard me using the same expression and wrote to correct me. She pointed out that it is space itself that is expanding, spreading out the mass of the universe. Most of that matter seems to have been inert or lifeless till about three and a half billion years ago, when the first self-replicating molecules came along and life began. Earth was dark with clouds that poured down rain, which fed the emerging seas. Spouted from erupting volcanoes, the earth's atmosphere was a mix of methane, ammonia, nitrogen, carbon dioxide and other gases that would poison most organisms today. Over millions of years these ingredients formed and reformed into countless random combinations. Scientists speculate that a combination of powerful natural forces, such as sunlight, geothermal heat, radioactivity and lightning, provided the critical jolts of energy that made the significant chemical reactions possible. The primal gene was probably a product of this chemical roulette, and the engine of biological evolution stuttered into action. Fifteen billion years after the Big Bang, humans came along and the universe started thinking about itself and, yes, knowing all that does put some of our pre-occupations into perspective, including what exactly we plan to have for dinner tonight.

Apart from marvelling at the fine-tuning of the universe that created the conditions in which the emergence of life and then consciousness could take place, the most immediate response I have to what we now know of the universe is shock at the prodigal waste and destruction that are such obvious features of its history. It is an appalling spectacle of explosive power simply barging its way through time and space. Some philosophers have described the life-force as a pure will to power that achieves in us the expression and consciousness of its own nature. Because we are creatures with aims, we ask about the purpose of this extraordinary process, but the universe itself gives us no answer and there may be none to give. Certainly, Nietzsche was convinced that the universe itself had no meaning: 'Becoming aims at nothing and achieves nothing,'[2] he wrote; it simply is. Even if we accept this, it does not mean that we ourselves are destined to lead pointless lives: we could hear it as a challenge to give our own lives meaning and purpose by the way we choose to act. Nevertheless, the waste and aimlessness of the universe can sicken and terrify us, and for those who want to believe in some kind of purpose behind it, its immense indifference is disturbing. The Russian poet Yevtushenko once asked the English novelist Kingsley Amis: 'You believe in God?' 'No,' he replied. 'Well, actually, it's more that I hate the bastard.'[3] And that hatred is another paradox: in us the universe expresses outrage at its own ugly indifference. Then another emerging paradox attracts our attention and finds a voice; human compassion. Here is a beautiful example of it from Glasgow's Poet Laureate, Edwin Morgan. It's his poem, 'In the Snack Bar'.

A cup capsizes along the formica,
slithering with a dull clatter.
A few heads turn in the crowded evening snack-bar.
An old man is trying to get to his feet
from the low round stool fixed to the floor.
Slowly he levers himself up, his hands have no power.
He is up as far as he can get. The dismal hump
looming over him forces his head down.
He stands in his stained beltless gaberdine
like a monstrous animal caught in a tent
in some story. He sways slightly,
the face not seen, bent down
in shadow under his cap.
Even on his feet he is staring at the floor
or would be, if he could see.
I notice now his stick, once painted white
but scuffed and muddy, hanging from his right arm.
Long blind, hunchback born, half paralysed
he stands
fumbling with his stick
and speaks:
'I want – to go to the – toilet.'
It is down two flights of stairs, but we go.

The poet assists him and describes the slow, complicated
descent to the lavatory in the basement and continues:

I set him in position, stand behind him
and wait with his stick.
His brooding reflection darkens the mirror
but the trickle of his water is thin and slow,
an old man's apology for living.
Painful ages to close his trousers and coat –
I do up the last buttons for him.

After helping him to wash and dry his hands, they start
climbing the stairs.

He climbs, and steadily enough.
He climbs, we climb. He climbs
with many pauses but with that one
persisting patience of the undefeated
which is the nature of man when all is said.
And slowly we go up. And slowly we go up.
The faltering, unfaltering steps
take him at last to the door
across the endless, yet not endless waste of floor.
I watch him helped on a bus. It shudders off in the rain.
The conductor bends to hear where he wants to go.

Wherever he could go it would be dark
and yet he must trust men.
Without embarrassment or shame
he must announce his most pitiful needs

in a public place. No one sees his face.
Does he know how frightening he is in his strangeness
under his mountainous coat, his hands like wet leaves
stuck to the half-white stick?
His life depends on many who would evade him.
But he cannot reckon up the chances,
having one thing to do,
to haul his blind hump through these rains of August.
Dear Christ, to be born for this![4]

In an aimless universe the emergence of compassion like that is an evolutionary miracle, a shock as remarkable as the sudden jump into life of the primal gene. And we can even give it an approximate date. We don't know much about humanity's earliest religious stirrings, but it's a pretty good guess that they were a projection of our own cloudy anxieties onto the blank mystery of the universe. In a brutal world, the first religious impulse was probably a combination of fear and uncertainty that gave rise to the cruelty of the sacrificial system and its placation of angry and unpredictable power. Arbitrary violence was clearly the nature of things. We know that in the animal community a position of power is achieved over the group by the dominant male, until he weakens and is replaced. The pecking or feeding-and-breeding order delivers a kind of balance to the group, though the threat of challenge to the existing order is never absent. Of course, the instinct to cooperate was also in there, and it may be the root from which human altruism has grown. Nevertheless, it was the powerful who ruled. This sheer will to power was something that Nietzsche said we must understand and even celebrate.

> Every enhancement of the type 'man' has so far been the work of an aristocratic society – and it will be so again and again – a society that believes in the long ladder of an order of rank and differences in value between man and man, and that needs slavery in some sense or other. Without that *pathos of distance* which grows out of the ingrained difference between strata – when the ruling caste constantly looks afar and looks down upon subjects and instruments and just as constantly practises obedience and command, keeping down and keeping at a distance – that other, more mysterious pathos could not have grown up either – the craving for an ever new widening of distances within the soul itself, the development of ever higher, rarer, more remote, further-stretching, more comprehensive states – in brief, simply the enhancement of the type 'man', the continual 'self-overcoming of man,' to use a moral formula in a supra-moral sense.

To be sure, one should not yield to humanitarian illusions about the origins of aristocratic society: truth is hard. Let us admit to ourselves, without trying to be considerate, how every higher culture on earth so far has *begun*. Human beings whose nature was still natural, barbarians in every terrible sense of the word, men of prey who were still in possession of unbroken strength of will and lust for power, hurled themselves upon weaker, more civilized, more peaceful races, perhaps traders or cattle raisers, or upon mellow old cultures whose last vitality was even then flaring up in splendid fireworks of spirit and corruption. In the beginning the noble caste was always the barbarian caste: their predominance did not lie mainly in physical strength but in strength of soul – they were more *whole* human beings (which also means, at every level, 'more whole beasts').[5]

That is the authentic voice of the will to power that seems to be intrinsic to the nature of the universe, the way things operate. There is no point in complaining about it, any more than it is worth moaning about the wetness of water or the hotness of fire. David Hume told us that you can't derive an 'ought' from an 'is', so there's little point in protesting about the way things seem to operate in this indifferent universe. Yet that is exactly what happened: voices of protest against the given order of things began to be heard and they bring us to another of those leaps in the evolution of the moral universe. These voices started calling out in various places and within various traditions during what is called the Axial Age from 800 to 200 BCE, one of the most extraordinary turning-points in human history. It was during this formative period that the chief civilisations began their separate development, yet on mysteriously parallel lines. There was a new prosperity everywhere that led to greater inequality and exploitation by the powerful of the weak. From within this universe of indifferent power rose a challenge to that power, as prophetic figures appeared who were no longer prepared to accept the way things were organised, and their voices were heard crying in the wilderness. In the Judeo-Christian tradition, we begin to hear that challenge from the prophets of the Hebrew Scriptures. Just remember that quote from Nietzsche about the men of power and the pathos of distance that placed them far above the pain and misery that seethed and struggled beneath them, and listen to these words from chapter 5 of the book of Amos, the Hebrew prophet of the eighth Century BCE:

[11] . . . because you trample on the poor
    and take from them levies of grain,
you have built houses of hewn stone,
    but you shall not live in them;
you have planted pleasant vineyards,
    but you shall not drink their wine.
[12] For I know how many are your transgressions,
    and how great are your sins –
you who afflict the righteous, who take a bribe,
    and push aside the needy in the gate.
[21] I hate, I despise your festivals,
    and I take no delight in your solemn assemblies.
[22] Even though you offer me your burnt offerings and
        grain offerings,
    I will not accept them;
and the offerings of well-being of your fatted animals
    I will not look upon.
[23] Take away from me the noise of your songs;
    I will not listen to the melody of your harps.
[24] But let justice roll down like waters,
    and righteousness like an ever-flowing stream.

The moral challenge to humankind that emerged during this period is known, in scholars' short-hand, as the birth of ethical monotheism and the very idea can come as a shock to some people. Was monotheism *unethical* before this? Let's just call it pre-moral, before the knowledge of good and evil. When invincible power is ruling, you don't challenge it, you humour and placate it. You flatter rulers, earthly or heavenly, you burn incense to them, pour out grain offerings and sacrifice fat beasts: that's what religion and politics were all about – until that extraordinary jump in human evolution that began to associate God, the supreme power in the universe, with the disgust felt by the prophets at the injustice that disfigured the earth. Humanity discovered the right-eousness of God, God's anger at oppression, God's pity for the poor. No matter how you interpret the origin of these claims, they represent an extraordin-ary human discovery: whether the insight came from God through the prophets to humanity or from humanity itself through prophets who thought it came from God, the fact is, it came. We invented or discovered conscience. The emergence of con-science and the birth of moral struggle seem to be the result of humanity's sundering from its animal past. We know that instincts that do not discharge themselves outwardly *turn inwards*. They do not cease with the emergence of conscience, but as society becomes more ordered and complex it is now rarely possible to gratify these instincts without losing the benefits and approval of the group, so they find new, subterranean satisfactions. The emergence of conscience would not be so painful if it had also brought moral power, if awareness of the greater good of the community brought the capacity always to choose the good, but that does not seem to be our experience. With the birth of conscience comes its twin, human discontent, and Freud is its most penetrating interpreter. It is probably a mistake to reckon that, at some point in history, humans got together with one another and entered into a social compact called civilisation that offered individuals the protection of the group at the price of the sacrifice of their personal autonomy. That, however, is how it seems to have worked out in practice and it does breed a kind of unease and discontent, particularly in powerful characters who feel constrained by the pressure of others to conform to the social norm. This was certainly how Freud interpreted the human predicament in 'The Future of an Illusion'. He discusses the fantasy we all flirt with from time to time of a life in which the renunciation of instinct is removed and the life-force is allowed to work in us without constraint in a pre-moral sort of way. This would involve, of course, the abandonment of civilisation. Freud comments:

But how ungrateful, how short-sighted after all, to strive for the abolition of civilization! What would then remain would be a state of nature, and that would be far harder to bear. It is true that nature would not demand any restrictions of instinct from us, she would let us do as we liked; but she has her own particularly effective method of restricting us. She destroys us – coldly, cruelly, relentlessly, as it seems to us, and possibly through the very things that occasioned our satisfaction. It was precisely because of these dangers with which nature threatens us that we came together and created civilization, which is also, among other things, intended to make our communal life possible. For the principal task of civilization, its actual raison d'être, is to defend us against nature.[6]

There are more optimistic ways of interpreting the human condition than through those two great prophets of suspicion, Nietzsche and Freud, but I would claim that there is much truth in their gloomy observation that in the emergence of what we might call intentional living from the pure flux of nature there also emerged a corresponding self-consciousness and sense of difficulty with ourselves. With the arrival of conscience came the human moral problematic: we suffer from ourselves, have become a problem to ourselves. The ancient myth in Genesis chapters 2 and 3 was written to express the human dilemma that was created by the knowledge of good and evil.

[15] The Lord God took the man and put him in the garden of Eden to till it and keep it. [16] And the Lord God commanded the man, 'You may freely eat of every tree of the garden; [17] but of the tree of the knowledge of good and evil you shall not eat, for in the day that you eat of it you shall die.' [3:1] Now the serpent was more crafty than any other wild animal that the Lord God had made. He said to the woman, 'Did God say, "You shall not eat from any tree in the garden"?' [2] The woman said to the serpent, 'We may eat of the fruit of the trees in the garden; [3] but God said, "You shall not eat of the fruit of the tree that is in the middle of the garden, nor shall you touch it, or you shall die."' [4] But the serpent said to the woman, 'You will not die; [5] for God knows that when you eat of it your eyes will be opened, and you will be like God, knowing good and evil.'

This ancient myth could be read as an account of the birth of reflective consciousness, when we fell from animal innocence into the knowledge of good and evil. The life-force of the universe still flows relentlessly through us, but now it is complicated by our attempts to direct and modify it in a more humane direction. Another way of describing our predicament was invented by Saint Paul, who called it the coming of the law. Julia Kristeva discusses Hannah Arendt's claim that it was St Paul who for the first time fully understood and expressed this fateful human dilemma. She writes, 'The Will, the interiority of the man-who-wills, and its ambivalence and intractable ambiguity all originate at the same time. It is impossible to satisfy the law, for our will to do so stimulates another will, the will to sin, and the one will is always accompanied by the other.'[7] This is an intended echo of Paul's Letter to the Romans chapter 7:

> . . . if it had not been for the law, I would not have known sin. I would not have known what it is to covet if the law had not said, 'You shall not covet.' [8] But sin, seizing an opportunity in the commandment, produced in me all kinds of covetousness . . . [15] I do not understand my own actions. For I do not do what I want, but I do the very thing I hate. [16] Now if I do what I do not want, I agree that the law is good. [17] But in fact it is no longer I that do it, but sin that dwells within me. [18] For I know that nothing good dwells within me, that is, in my flesh. I can will what is right, but I cannot do it. [19] For I do not do the good I

want, but the evil I do not want is what I do. [20] Now if I do what I do not want, it is no longer I that do it, but sin that dwells within me. [21] So I find it to be a law that when I want to do what is good, evil lies close at hand. [22] For I delight in the law of God in my inmost self, [23] but I see in my members another law at war with the law of my mind, making me captive to the law of sin that dwells in my members. [24] Wretched man that I am! Who will rescue me from this body of death?'

This is the cause of the greatest pain our humanity carries, the fact and remembrance of our own failures, those acts that can never be undone or reversed, which now turn the past into a great weight of regret that we bear everywhere with us and cannot lay down. Just as a stopped clock can bear permanent witness to the exact time of a particular atrocity, so the memory of a particular event in our past can have the power to close off the future and stop our life. And it is not just the memory of our own misdeeds that halts us in life; being a victim of someone else's evil act can be even more immobilising. One of the ways the human animal has learnt to deal with the pain of the past is by burying it behind a fog of denial. It is as though we know instinctively that if we look too closely at the thing that was done to us it will completely paralyse us, so we hide it from ourselves like a mad relative in the back room of the basement. But its presence down there leaches into our lives anyway, affecting our relationships and our general conduct in ways we ourselves probably never fully comprehend.

It is this failed attempt to deny the power of the past upon our lives that, paradoxically, may offer the clue to our healing. Another clue can be found in the way certain strong natures seem to break the normal human pattern and are able to disregard those who have offended them and move on. Nietzsche, because he was a profound psychologist who was fascinated by strong characters, is better on this subject than almost anyone I have ever read. He knew better than anyone how the past can rob us of the future and how our lives can be stunted by remembrance and sorrow. But he was also a celebrant of those he described as possessing strong, full natures who were incapable of taking their enemies or even their own misdeeds seriously for very long, because they had a powerful innate ability to recuperate and forget.[8] In an early essay on the use and abuse of history he writes:

> In order to determine the extent and thereby the
> boundary point at which past things must be forgotten

if they are not to become the grave diggers of the present, one has to know the exact extent of the plastic energy of a person, of a people, of a culture; that is, the power to grow uniquely from within, to transform and incorporate the past and the unknown, to heal wounds, to replace what is lost, and to duplicate shattered structures from within . . . There are people so lacking this energy that they bleed to death, as if from a tiny scratch, after a single incident, a single pain, and often in particular a single minor injustice.[9]

The other philosopher who thought deeply about this was Hannah Arendt. She meditated on how the past has the power to deny us the future, by imprisoning us in our own irreversible actions.

And this is the simple fact that, though we don't know what we are doing when we are acting, we have no possibility ever to undo what we have done. Action processes are not only unpredictable, they are also irreversible; there is no author or maker who can undo, destroy, what he has done if he does not like it or when the consequences are disastrous. The possible redemption from the predicament of irreversibility is the faculty of forgiving, and the remedy for unpredictability is contained in the faculty to make and keep promises. The two remedies belong together: forgiving relates to the past and serves to undo its deeds, while binding oneself through promises serves to set up in the ocean of future uncertainty islands of security without which not even continuity, let alone durability of any kind, would ever be possible in the relationships between men. Without being forgiven, released from the consequences of what we have done, our capacity to act would, as it were, be confined to one single deed from which we could never recover; we would remain the victim of its consequences for ever, not unlike the sorcerer's apprentice who lacked the magic formula to break the spell. Without being bound to the fulfilment of promises, we would never be able to achieve that amount of identity and continuity which together produce the 'person' about whom a story can be told; each of us would be condemned to wander helplessly and without direction in the darkness of his own lonely heart, caught in its ever changing moods, contradictions, and equivocalities. In this respect, forgiving and making promises are like control mechanisms built into the very faculty to start new and unending processes.[10]

I want to leave till the last chapter a consideration of what, if anything, we can do about the kind of monstrous evils that seem to be humanly beyond the reach of Hannah Arendt's formula of promise and forgiveness, deeds that Derrida would call 'unforgivable'. Our day-to-day problems with one another do not usually reach that horrifying dimension, though they are bad enough and can destroy our happiness. It gets most of the publicity, but the fact remains that real evil done by one person to another is rarer than the good deeds that attract no publicity. That is why Hannah Arendt is more concerned with what she calls 'trespasses', those everyday breaks in the harmony of life or tears in the web of human relationships, than with monstrous evils. If we are not to be immobilised by these everyday offences, then we have to learn to forgive each other in order for life to go on. The way she advises us to do this is to focus not on the act or the trespass, but on the person who committed it, because forgiveness is al-ways of individuals, never of actions. We cannot ever forgive a murder or a theft, but we might learn to forgive a murderer or a thief. According to Arendt, 'By being aimed at *someone* and not *something,* forgiveness becomes an act of love.'[11] We have not yet reached the level of Derrida's impossible forgiveness of the unfor-givable, but the need to forgive each other our tres-passes if we are to reclaim the future is difficult enough to manage. The fundamental insight here is that we can and must retain an attitude of disgust towards the offending act, if we are to justify the legitimate claims of human justice; nevertheless, we must find a way of preventing these irreversible offences from locking us permanently into the past; and the remedy for this dilemma is forgiveness of the person, not of what the person has done. When we begin to explore how to manage this quite complex manoeuvre, we discover that, over the years, we have created sophisticated systems that help us to deal effectively with the harm we do to one another. In the next chapter, I shall look at some of the techniques we have developed to help us manage the chaos that we so often make of our own lives.

CHAPTER THREE

Managing the Chaos

Finding the right title for a book is an art. Some good books have lousy titles and some good titles are fig leaves over bad books. One of the best book titles I have ever come across was by John Stewart Collis, a popular writer about science and nature. The title was *The Worm Forgives the Plough*. I never read the book, but I fancied I knew what it was about, because it had a title that immediately communicated a strong idea. I assumed the book was about the symbiosis of the natural world, its ecological connectedness. Of course, it is an example of the sympathetic fallacy to imagine that the worm actively and intentionally forgives the plough as it is being sliced in half, but it's not hard to get the idea. Nature is a great food chain and all living creatures live off and depend upon one another. That is the inescapable reality of things, but there is a tragic grandeur to it, suggesting that we are all part of a great system of sacrifice and mutuality.

Recently I watched a marvellous television nature

programme about animals in the high mountain regions of Africa. One of the shots was of a mountain leopard waiting, quivering with attention, above a mole hill, ready to pounce when the little blind creature reached the surface. With one fierce thrust of the head it had the mole in its jaw, the neck instantly broken. It is not only animals who feed off one another: humans are part of the same interdependent chain of being. It is easy to forget this in an urban culture that insulates us against the facts of our own dependence on nature and the animal kingdom. We see it more clearly in communities that live closer to the earth than the rest of us. One of the reasons for the tension between town and country over hunting is that each group has a different cultural experience. Country people often accuse town dwellers of hypocrisy, of weeping over cruelty to foxes, while ignoring the miserable existence of the battery hens and Christmas turkeys they happily buy at their local supermarkets.

Two poems capture, for me, the tragic symbiosis of nature and our part in it. The first, about hunters, is by Rebecca West:

We are all bowmen in this place.
The pattern of the birds against the sky
Our arrows overprint, and then they die.

But it is also common to our race
That when the birds fall down we weep.
Reason's a thing we dimly see in sleep.[1]

The other one, 'Praise of a Collie' by Norman Mac-
Caig, is both tender and shocking:

She was a small dog, neat and fluid –
Even her conversation was tiny:
She greeted you with *bow*, never *bow-wow*.

Her sons stood monumentally over her
But did what she told them. Each grew grizzled
Till it seemed he was his own mother's grandfather.

Once, gathering sheep on a showery day,
I remarked how dry she was. Pollóchan said, 'Ah,
It would take a very accurate drop to hit Lassie.'

She sailed in the dinghy like a proper sea-dog.
Where's a burn? – she's first on the other side.
She flowed through fences like a piece of black wind.

But suddenly she was old and sick and crippled . . .
I grieved for Pollóchan when he took her a stroll
And put the gun to the back of her head.[2]

That is the way of all the earth. The pain of consciousness is that we have projected our own emotions on to
the indifferent processes of nature and embroidered it
with our own sense of loss and tragedy. We are
compulsive anthropomorphisers who read our own
pain and sorrow into the lives of other species. Nevertheless, there can be a mysterious comfort in accepting
the nature of a universe in which the worm is crushed
by the grieving plough and in which hunters weep over
the beauty of the birds they slaughter. There's an
astonishingly moving meditation right at the end of
Camus' *The Outsider*, when the condemned man Meur-
sault lies on the bunk in his prison cell:

> I must have had a longish sleep, for, when I woke, the
> stars were shining down on my face. Sounds of the
> countryside came faintly in, and the cool night air,
> veined with smells of earth and salt, fanned my cheeks.
> The marvellous peace of the sleepbound summer
> night flooded through me like a tide . . . gazing up
> at the dark sky spangled with its signs and stars, for the
> first time, the first, I laid my heart open to the benign
> indifference of the universe.[3]

I would like to suggest that this mood of acceptance of
the benign indifference of the world is close to the
springs of what we mean by forgiveness. Fatalism is not

[42]

quite the right word here, though Nietzsche told us to love fate, to have what he called *amor fati*, to say yes to the unavoidable necessity of things. The normal sense of the word fatalism is too passive for the experience I am trying to uncover. The mood I am after is more celebratory than resigned. It actively says yes to the tragic reality of life, including the facts of pain and loss. Two instinctive responses lie behind this affirmation: that there is, first of all, a wise, sometimes rueful, awareness that the universe is bigger than us and will get us all in the end; and, secondly, that to completely understand any human act, including what we would describe as a wicked act, we would have to know all the facts of the universe. To know all would be to forgive all, to know all would be to accept the necessity of the worm-crushing plough and the need for hunters to feed their young, not to mention all the other ways in which we exploit one another. We have to begin our search for understanding and wisdom by accepting that in the great chain of being all effects have causes that are themselves the effects of causes that were effected by causes, going back all the way to that mysterious uncaused cause we call the Big Bang. This is not quite the same thing as saying that everything is so absolutely mechanistically determined that there is no point in judging people for the way they act. Though it is true that we all tend to judge too quickly, it seems to be intrinsic to our nature to discriminate between types of conduct, some of which we blame, some of which we praise. What we are less good at recognising is that the scope of human freedom is surprisingly slight and fragile. An understanding of this may lie behind Hannah Arendt's distinction between the need to forgive the person who has wounded us, while continuing to condemn what the person has done. This is a difficult balance to sustain, but it seems to be important to hold these two apparently opposing values in some kind of equilibrium: the need to reclaim the future for humanity by forgiving its offenders, by refusing to let their past actions simply stop time, as it were, and freeze it at a particular moment of passion or madness or carelessness or forgetfulness or confusion; while, at the same time, retaining the moral ability to identify the actions themselves as bad, as things that should never have been done.

There is a tragic fact here that needs to be faced. The reason we want to be able to forgive individuals, while retaining the important ability to judge their actions, is that we know that personal action is the fruit of character and that character is largely predetermined by factors that are not in our control. The most tragic contemporary version of this hideous dilemma is the sexual abuse of children. Apart from the kind of opportunist sexual use of children that may sometimes be an outlet for ordinary adult lust, most compulsive abusers seem to have been made that way by external circumstances. We know that many, if not all, abusers were themselves abused from an early age. We know that they are emotionally fixated on children. We know that they persuade themselves that the relations they have with children are freely consented to. Sexual abuse of children is at the extreme end of our tolerance meter, but it does illustrate the tragic dilemma that faces a human being whose character has been formed in a way that is totally unacceptable to the rest of the human community. Actions are the result of character and our characters seem to be stamped upon us from the beginning, like a kind of predestined fate, for good or evil. It is theoretically possible to reform or remould the character into a different pattern, but major developmental changes rarely seem to occur in the human psyche. The most we can usually hope for is the strength to develop avoidance strategies that may help us to manage our compulsions in less destructive ways. Nevertheless, extraordinary transformations do sometimes occur.

I once had a discussion with a scholarly psychiatrist about the offending behaviour of the violent young men who tragically pack our prisons. We agreed that most of these men had been formed by circumstances beyond their control. Can nothing be done with or for them? I asked. Yes, he said, we can work to change the determinants, the factors that produce or influence our conduct. We know that this can lead to profound behavioural change in characters that appear to be already formed beyond reformation. There are many stories of tough and violent men whose lives were radically redirected by altering the circumstances that determined their conduct. By educating them, by increasing their self-worth and thereby enabling their enormous energy to express itself in positive, sometimes artistic ways, amazing changes can occur, as several notable examples from within the recent history of Scotland's hard men will prove. I once sat in on a group session at Grendon Prison for major offenders and saw this process at work. The men were all serious criminals serving life sentences. They had applied to join this therapeutic community because they had all reached a point, after years in prison, at which they wanted to alter the pattern of their own behaviour and change the inner determinants of their characters. Observing the dialectic that operated in that brutally honest group session was fascinating. A fundamental element in the process was that they had to acknowledge and own the reality of the terrible things they had done, while, at the same time and without turning it into an excuse, they had to recognise that they themselves had been moulded by circumstances that were not in their control. What made the difference, what gave them back the future, was the decision to try to take control of their own destiny, probably for the first time in their lives. Part of the process involved a radical kind of self-forgiveness that meant accepting the way the universe had formed them. This was dynamic forgiveness in action, but the interesting thing to note about it was that it was almost entirely contained within the drama of the offender's own life. So far, we have not brought the victim onto the stage. As a matter of fact, part of the process of rehabilitation for major criminals probably ought to involve carefully organised encounters with their victims, if each consents to the process. This would mean a switch from retributive justice, pure punishment, to restorative justice, which is based on the concept of reparation. Reparation repairs the damage done by the crime, either by some act of material restoration, such as payment or service, or by some kind of symbolic gesture such as willingness to cooperate in special programmes of training or therapy.

Creative forgiveness can have a life-changing impact

on all the actors in the tragedies of humanity, but I want to stick with offenders for the moment. What we are looking for is the injection of a dynamic force into the logjam that will get the clogged river moving again: in the case of the offender, something that will break up and re-form the character that is locked in certain patterns of destructive habit. There are many human arenas where this process can begin. For example, the emphasis on self-acceptance leading to self-forgiveness, which will, in turn, lead to personal change, is a fundamental part of psycho-therapy. In the language of person-centred therapy, the counsellor offers the client empathy and unconditional positive regard, no matter what is being revealed. This creates a space of safety where the client, often burdened with guilt and self-hatred, is able to see himself or herself as a creature caught in the web of being, who has acted, however badly, from within a particular history that is itself part of a larger history that is part of all history. I read somewhere that the origins of the First World War of 1914–18 could be traced back to the building of the Great Wall of China more than 2,000 years earlier. Chou en Lai made a similar point when he said that it was still too early to know whether the French Revolution had been successful. Behind these sweeping claims lies the assumption that human history is

connected or joined-up, so to make particular judg-
ments about parts of the process is always going to be
inaccurate and incomplete. The same point was made
by many commentators after September 11, 2001:
terrorists are bred by circumstances, they do not come
fully formed from the womb of hell; they are made by
history not Satan. So are we all, which is why we must
all learn the art of forgiving, and the hardest place to
start is in the struggle with our own guilt.

We are all different from each other, of course, but
most of us seem to be quite good at forgiving or
understanding human weakness in people we love, at
sticking with our friends through the painful consequences of their mistakes. It is much more difficult to
apply the same generosity to ourselves. I have often
quoted Hopkins to people who were held in the vice of
self-loathing:

> My own heart let me more have pity on; let
> Me live to my sad self hereafter kind,
> Charitable; not live this tormented mind
> With this tormented mind tormenting yet.[4]

Sometimes the self-hatred amounts to the complete
rejection of what is perceived to have been a worthless
life. This is certainly the mood behind some lacerating
words about old age in T. S. Eliot's *Little Gidding*:

And last, the rending pain of re-enactment
of all that you have done and been; the shame
of motives late revealed, and the awareness
of things ill done and done to others' harm
which once you took for exercise of virtue.[5]

I have frequently encountered this mood in the elderly; it is the most saddening aspect of old age, 'the rending pain of re-enactment of all that you have done and been'. There is an inevitable tendency in people, when they look back on their lives, to concentrate on their failures and mistakes, wrong roads taken, right roads not taken. That is when shame burns, and people are tempted to feel that they have done little or nothing with the time they were given. It may be that the great monsters of human history ought to feel this kind of shame but, generally speaking, wallowing in this sort of guilt is pointless and shows an ungrateful lack of balance. I shall come to the positive side of confession in a moment, but it has to be admitted that there has been a tendency in the Christian tradition to over-emphasise human sinfulness, which is why penitence has had a disproportionate role in liturgy and private devotion. It is easy to get this business out of balance, the way newspapers do when they endlessly report bad news, because bad news is good news from their point of view, while good news is no news. My confessor once ordered me, after a particularly mournful confession of my sins, to come back next time and make a confession of thanksgiving for the things I had managed to do well. Knowledge of our failings is important if we are to live the examined life, but complete honesty will involve finding the balance between our good points and our bad. In any case, the real motive for self-examination is not so that we can beat ourselves up for being miserable sinners, but so that we can grow in self-knowledge and manage our relationships a bit more wisely. We should be honest about what we have done badly, but we should also acknowledge what we have done well in our journey through life. Most lives are achievements that have had their share of sorrow and endurance. The point I am making here is that we have to bring to the examined life a kind of objectivity that enables us to look at ourselves with compassionate impartiality.

If forgiving ourselves is difficult enough, finding the energy to forgive others can be almost impossible. This can lead to an excruciating double bind, in which our inability to forgive adds guilt to the pain that is already in our souls, because now we have to acknowledge that we continue to hold grudges, can't let things go and walk away, but endlessly proceed from wrong to wrong like a rat caught in a cage. This is Eliot's 'rending pain of re-enactment' with a vengeance. Listening to people caught in this predicament makes one painfully aware of how apt the trapped-animal analogy is. At the root of the word 'obsession' is the Latin for being under siege and that is what this state of mind feels like. Compulsive obsessive disorders are wrackingly repetitive, as the mind drives the body through endless rituals and routines without surcease. The inability to forgive and let go can feel like that. The offence, the assault upon the body or soul of the victim, is endlessly reprised. The details of the insult or brutality or infidelity are exhaustively rehearsed to anyone who will listen, and the mind and heart are permanently under siege as memory plays the injury over and over, just the way TV endlessly repeats news clips of catastrophes, like those shots of the hijacked planes plunging into the Twin Towers in Manhattan. If these public tragedies can play endlessly in our minds, think of the undying effect on people of hurt that violated their trust in others. It is the destruction of trust that is the damning thing here, except that it is the victim who suffers damnation, as the abuse is relived or the memory of the broken promise runs round the mind in a loop that nothing seems able to stop.

We must apply exactly the same strategy to the guilt

of the victim who cannot forgive as we did to the guilt of the offender who seeks forgiveness: unconditional positive regard, deep understanding and an honest acknowledgment that this is the way things are and that they have been made that way by factors that are not in the person's control. We only add to the trauma if we try to urge or hurry people into a forgiveness they are humanly incapable of offering. We find an eloquent example of this in the South African Truth Commission. In the essay from which I have already quoted, Derrida tells us that Archbishop Tutu recounted how one day a black woman came to testify before the Commission. Her husband had been tortured then killed by police officers. She speaks in one of the eleven languages officially recognised by the Commission, and Archbishop Tutu, who seems to speak them all, translates her words in this way: 'A commission or a government cannot forgive. Only I, eventually, could do it. (And I am not ready to forgive.)'[6] It is possible to acknowledge the fact that only the act of forgiveness can release the victim from the treadmill of the past, while understanding how humanly impossible it is to grant that forgiveness. We have to say an unconditional yes to the inability to forgive; indeed, we may have to go further and acknowledge the appropriate moral force of the refusal to forgive and the sense of revulsion that the very thought of forgiveness induces in the victim. For parents even to begin to imagine forgiving the man who has stalked, abducted, violated and murdered their beloved six-year-old daughter, whose remembered smile still breaks their hearts, is against every good and natural impulse of their being.

This is why the severe conditionality that we sometimes hear in the words of Jesus about forgiveness begins to jar with us, such as these verses from Matthew, chapter 6: '[14] For if you forgive others their trespasses, your heavenly Father will also forgive you; [15] but if you do not forgive others, neither will your Father forgive your trespasses.' We could perhaps take some of the harshness out of that text by observing that it is an observable truth that the inability or refusal to forgive can be a sentence of psychic imprisonment that locks the person for ever into the remembrance of the original trespass. Just as forgiveness gives the offender the capacity to move away from the moment of trespass and regain the future; so the victim's inability to forgive makes it impossible for her to move on into the future. I cannot read the conditionality in these words of Jesus as anything other than tragically descriptive: we cannot order people to forgive, but we can recognise that their inability to forgive may have the tragic effect of binding them to the past and condemning them to a life-sentence of bitterness. Sometimes there is a strength and grandeur in the refusal to forgive. Something of this comes through the words of the woman who spoke to the Truth Commission and it is certainly what we find in the great Nazi hunter Simon Wiesenthal, who dedicated his whole life to the unforgiving search for those who were responsible for the murder of millions of his people. The refusal to forgive can be the righteous thing to do, the thing that justice commands. Nevertheless, the fact remains that the inability or refusal to forgive, though it may be morally appropriate, always extends the reign of the original sin into the future, so that it can end up dominating a whole life or the life of a whole people.

We see this process pitilessly at work in those chronic ethnic and religious feuds that sentence generations of people to decades, sometimes centuries, of bitterness and bloodshed. In our own era, the most emblematic example of humanity's capacity for trapping itself in chronic and intractable conflict is provided by the violence that has surrounded the State of Israel since its inception half a century ago. It had been the tragic fate of the Jewish people to be scattered throughout the earth for centuries, persecuted and despised wherever they settled. And it was in Christian Europe in the twentieth century that the monstrous decision was taken to try to rid them from the earth. The longing to return to Palestine, in order to escape from their long and bitter exile, gave birth to Zionism and the violent emergence of the State of Israel. The tragedy was that the return of one lost people to their ancient homeland created a new exiled community, the Palestinians. Every day we witness the terrible wounds these crucified communities inflict on each other, with neither side able to feel the other's pain. Neither community seems capable of forgiving the past in order to discover a new and better future. It appears that they would rather go on dying separately than try to learn to live alongside each other. I shall spend more time in the next chapter exploring this intractably unforgiving element in human nature; for the moment I simply want to note the painful paradoxes inherent in both the command and the refusal to forgive.

The saying of Jesus about the need to forgive others if we are ourselves to be forgiven, seems to stress the conditional nature of forgiveness in the life of the person who has been offended: if we are not prepared to forgive those who have trespassed against us, then the time will surely come when we ourselves will be denied the forgiveness we need. As someone once put it, our previous refusal to forgive will have destroyed the bridge we ourselves now need to cross. But conditional forgiveness has a slightly different meaning when it is applied to the sinner seeking forgiveness. Here the conditionality expresses itself through the demand for repentance followed by confession, before forgiveness is granted. This way of managing the mechanics of forgiveness is very clear in the Christian tradition, but it is also a strong human instinct: we expect people to own up to what they have done, especially during those spectacles we all enjoy so much today, when a well-known figure, such as a politician, has been caught in a trespass against the code of public life. People who earn their living advising our leaders on managing these situations always say that it is best, if they are guilty, to own up immediately and make a clean breast of it. I am always embarrassed at the way they are also encouraged to abase themselves and express boundless sorrow for the offence, as though the public were the victim of the trespass. There must be a way of being honest about a fault without indulging in that kind of public abasement, but it does not seem to be a part of the confessional ritual of public life at the moment. Behind these ordeals of televised humiliation there lies an element of the truth I have been circling in this chapter: the best way to stop the impact of a particular act from thrusting into the rest of our lives and stealing the future from us is to acknowledge it and, by confession and absolution, cut off its power to metastasise. This is the wisdom that lies behind the Christian tradition of the confession of sin. Confession may have been over-emphasised in church and may have drained a lot of psychic energy from believers, who had to spend so much time avoiding the bad and examining themselves to see if they had fallen into it that they had little energy left for actively pursuing the good. The fact that Jesus seemed to think that outcasts and sinners were usually more loving than the virtuous was probably because, having given up the struggle against the sins of the flesh, they had more energy left to tackle the more deadly sins of the spirit. While all that may be true, it has been wise of Christianity to insist that confession is good for the soul. Here is how the first chapter of the First Letter of John puts it: '[8] If we say that we have no sin, we deceive ourselves, and the truth is not in us. [9] If we confess our sins, he who is faithful and just will forgive us our sins and cleanse us from all unrighteousness.'

The conditionality of forgiveness was the basis for the emergence of the discipline of private confession in the Christian tradition. Inevitably, it became too forensic and intrusive over the years. By making it compulsory before the reception of holy communion, the Church trivialised it and weakened its particular usefulness to souls heavily burdened with guilt. Nevertheless, through a ritual of repentance leading to the authoritative pronouncement of absolution, confession has provided a practical method of release for troubled souls for centuries. The fact that the practice still goes on in different ways, though the confessionals in church have been largely abandoned, is testimony to the efficacy of the process itself, whether it is done through a priest, a psycho-therapist or your best friend in the pub after a drink too many. It is the instinct to look at what we have made of ourselves and try, before it is too late, to do something about it. And Jesus still has some of the best words for it:

There was a man who had two sons. [12] The younger of them said to his father, 'Father, give me the share of the property that will belong to me.' So he divided his property between them. [13] A few days later the younger son gathered all he had and travelled to a distant country, and there he squandered his property in dissolute living. [14] When he had spent everything, a severe famine took place throughout that country, and he began to be in need. [15] So he went and hired himself out to one of the citizens of that country, who sent him to his fields to feed the pigs. [16] He would gladly have filled himself with the pods that the pigs were eating; and no one gave him anything. [17] But when he came to himself he said, 'How many of my father's hired hands have bread enough and to spare, but here I am dying of hunger! [18] I will get up and go to my father, and I will say to him, "Father, I have sinned against heaven and before you; [19] I am no longer worthy to be called your son; treat me like one of your hired hands." ' [20] So he set off and went to his father.

The traditional way to read the parable of the prodigal son is to interpret it as an example of conditional forgiveness at work, through the process of repentance, leading to confession, followed by re-instatement. The focus is usually on the moment of self-realisation when the wayward son 'came to himself' and decided to go to his father and confess the sin he had committed. This moment of repentance, which means a radical change of mind, is the act that triggers forgiveness. Behind it is the theory that you cannot receive or make active use of forgiveness until you acknowledge that you need it. A moment spent reflecting on the psychological phenomenon known as 'denial' seems to be relevant here. As long as we go on denying that we have a problem with something that is actually disabling us we are not in a position to deal with it. The purpose of coming to ourselves and admitting our true condition is so that we can start dealing with the difficulty and stop running away from it. Repentance followed by confession is the sequence that opens us to the changing power of forgiveness. I, as the victim, may already have forgiven you and moved on, but unless you can admit to the trespass the value of my forgiveness will lie there like an uncashed cheque.

That is still the most usual way to read this parable and the theory of forgiveness that has been based upon it. Repentance is change of heart and mind. It acknowledges the reality of what we have done, the kind of persons we are. It is a radical honesty that comes as an enormous relief to the troubled spirit; it is the moment when we stop running from the truth about ourselves. It is normally the prelude to a new kind of self-management that begins by confessing and trying to repair the damage we have done to others in the past. Like the prodigal son, we come to ourselves and go to the one we have hurt and confess our fault. But there is another, more radical, reading of this parable that may provide a clue to understanding my epigraph from Derrida. I want to add to that conundrum a further paradox that reverses the normal order of repentance followed by confession: there is a kind of forgiveness that is so absolute and unconditional that it can create repentance in the heart that has been hardened against change. Although the path of conditional forgiveness – the path of repentance, confession and re-instatement – is the one we follow most commonly in our daily relations with each other, I want in the next chapter to explore the experience of unconditional forgiveness, a forgiveness so total and so generous that it can sometimes redirect the path of history.

CHAPTER FOUR

Redeeming the Chaos

In the previous chapter I looked at some of the ways in which we have tried to manage the chaos we make of our lives. After much bitter experience, we create various salvage systems to repair the damage we do to one another, often blindly and ignorantly. I suggested that, because we are largely programmed by factors over which we have little control and about which we are sometimes in complete ignorance, we often trespass upon each other in ways that can interrupt or completely stop the movement and enjoyment of life. A single act of passion or thoughtlessness can destroy someone's future happiness. The possibilities are too numerous to list except in a generic sort of way, such as the driver who has one drink too many and destroys a young life, thereby plunging himself into life-long guilt and the family of the dead child into life-long grief; the act of adultery that destroys a long marriage and tears apart the parents of children who love them both; the word spoken in anger that we wish we could immediately take back, but which continues to reverberate destructively in the lives of those we love. It is almost certain that we have also offended in ways we were unaware of at the time, but they go on damaging the hearts and minds of people whom we have long since forgotten. That is one reason why, in one of the acts of sacramental confession used in church, penitents confess sins that they 'cannot now remember', knowing that the effect of what they have ignorantly said or done may still be eating away at someone's soul. One of the things that most depressed me when I went out visiting parishioners as a priest was the frequency with which I encountered people who would rehearse in minute detail incidents from decades ago that had scarred their souls. Though often surprisingly trivial, the continuing impact of these events was powerful. Frequently the offences were committed by professional carers, such as clergy, who had thoughtlessly dropped an inappropriate remark into their conversation or engaged in inappropriate behaviour at some painful moment in the person's life, and the experience had gone into them like a knife, creating a wound that had never healed.

If these individual misdeeds or acts of carelessness are difficult enough to deal with or recover from, much worse are the crimes that groups have inflicted upon each other. The original sin may have been committed hundreds of years earlier, but it still scars the collective consciousness of whole communities and keeps them imprisoned in the past. I have already made reference to the conflict in Israel/Palestine; another example would be the continuing impact of the memory of slavery on race relations in the United States. Applying the confessional technique that we have been looking at to these situations is incredibly difficult. The place where it has been tried most systematically is in South Africa with the Truth Commission. Probably because of the powerful influence of Christians like Archbishop Tutu, the mechanics of conditional forgiveness have been tried there with some success. Amnesty, the political equivalent of forgiveness and absolution, was extended to those who admitted or confessed their trespasses during the bitter years of apartheid. It is hard not to admire this attempt to apply the theology of conditional forgiveness to such an intractable human situation and even more difficult not to wish it well.

The premise on which the system of conditional forgiveness is based is the principle of personal responsibility: A did X; X was a harmful act; A admits responsibility for the offence and is forgiven. The prodigal son insults his father by claiming his inheritance and adds injury to insult by wasting it in riotous living. He 'comes to himself', goes back and confesses his sin to his father, who forgives and re-instates him. What is happening when forgiveness operates in such a situation? More importantly, what does it mean to the parties involved in the conflict? I suspect that behind it there is an attempt to impose some kind of order and rationality on the chaos our conduct has created. But how does admitting responsibility and expressing sorrow alter the impact of an event that is itself irreversible? The act and its consequences *cannot* be undone, but confession may change the psychological reaction of the victim to the event and interrupt the expected sequence of revenge. We seem to have a wired-in instinct for retributive justice, for getting even with those who cause us hurt. If we are too weak to take straightforward revenge, we sometimes find surreptitious ways of getting back at our tormentors. In the 1991 movie *Frankie and Johnny*, featuring Al Pacino and Michelle Pfeiffer, we watch harassed waiters in a busy Manhattan diner avenging themselves against bullying customers by doing unmentionable things to their burgers before pouring on the ketchup. Harder to deal with are the situations where no vindication for the hurt has been possible, probably because of an imbalance in the power relations between the parties. This is where we are most likely to meet the person suffering from a chronic sense of grievance whose only method of relief may be the continuous rehearsal of the story to anyone who will listen. It is because we recognise the corrosive effect of this kind of victimisation on people that we have instituted laws against sexual and racial harassment and unfair dismissal. All this is complicated enough when the offences are relatively trivial; it gets progressively more difficult as the seriousness of the trespass increases. The psycho-analyst Adam Phillips has interesting things to say about the hurt and anger we feel when we are abused or trespassed upon. He writes:

> Our angers are inarticulate theories of justice; they are articulated, acted out, in revenge. Revenge, one might say, is the genre of rage. If rage renders us helpless, revenge gives us something to do. It organizes our disarray. It is one way of making the world, or one's life, make sense. Revenge turns rupture into story. And it shows us the extent to which meaning is complicit with the possibility of redress, with a belief that losses can be made good (revenge as savagely optimistic mourning). Because tragedy always threatens to baffle the possibility of action – our minor tragedies, as well as real ones – revenge keeps hope alive.[1]

It was to bring some kind of order into the volatile situations created by human anger at injuries against the person that Moses created the law of proportionate response in Exodus, chapter 21.

[12] Whoever strikes a person mortally shall be put to death. [13] If it was not premeditated, but came about by an act of God, then I will appoint for you a place to which the killer may flee. [14] But if someone willfully attacks and kills another by treachery, you shall take the killer from my altar for execution. [18] When individuals quarrel and one strikes the other with a stone or fist so that the injured party, though not dead, is confined to bed, [19] but recovers and walks around outside with the help of a staff, then the assailant shall be free of liability, except to pay for the loss of time, and to arrange for full recovery. [20] When a slave owner strikes a male or female slave with a rod and the slave dies immediately, the owner shall be punished. [21] But if the slave survives a day or two, there is no punishment; for the slave is the owner's property. [22] When people who are fighting injure a pregnant woman so that there is a miscarriage, and yet no further harm follows, the one responsible shall be fined what the woman's husband demands, paying as much as the judges determine. [23] If any harm

follows, then you shall give life for life, [24] eye for eye, tooth for tooth, hand for hand, foot for foot, [25] burn for burn, wound for wound, stripe for stripe.

This kind of ordered and proportionate response to injury was designed to limit the reaction to the kind of incidents that, if not dealt with adequately, can escalate into feuds that endure for generations. One of the most outrageous things that Jesus ever attempted was to replace this sane and carefully calibrated response to injustice with a system of non-resistance.

[38] You have heard that it was said, 'An eye for an eye and a tooth for a tooth.' [39] But I say to you, Do not resist an evildoer. But if anyone strikes you on the right cheek, turn the other also; [40] and if anyone wants to sue you and take your coat, give your cloak as well; [41] and if anyone forces you to go one mile, go also the second mile. [42] Give to everyone who begs from you, and do not refuse anyone who wants to borrow from you. [43] You have heard that it was said, 'You shall love your neighbour and hate your enemy.' [44] But I say to you, Love your enemies and pray for those who persecute you, [45] so that you may be children of your Father in heaven; for he makes his sun rise on the evil and on the good, and sends rain on the righteous and on the unrighteous.

These words from the Sermon on the Mount in Matthew chapter 5 do not seem to be consistent with the teaching of Jesus on conditional forgiveness that we looked at in the last chapter, but I am less interested in trying to establish some sort of systematic consistency in Jesus than in trying to figure out what is humanly going on when we suppress our instinct for revenge and try to offer unconditional forgiveness to those who have offended us, no matter how brutally. George Steiner is interesting here. He describes the law of Moses as the first great attempt to impose some sort of moral order on humanity. We probably ought to reject the claim that it was the first serious attempt to order the unruly affairs of humanity, but we can acknowledge that it was certainly one of the most thoughtful and carefully articulated. We have already noticed that it is based on a system of proportionality, whereby revenge is carefully calibrated to fit the seriousness of the crime. Steiner writes:

> The profoundly natural impulse to avenge injustice, oppression and derision do have their place in the house of Israel. A refusal to forget injury or humiliation can warm the heart. Christ's ordinance of total love, of self-offering to the assailant, is, in any strict sense, an enormity. The victim is to love his butcher. A

monstrous proposition. But one shedding fathomless light. How are mortal men and women to fulfil it?[2]

Before asking how we could fulfil this kind of impossible forgiveness we must first try to figure out what kind of moral basis, if any, it might have. Is the abandonment of the traditional penalty system of proportional response a moral advance on the Mosaic law, supposing it were possible to follow it in the first place? I wonder whether the clue lies in another of Jesus' parables, found in Matthew chapter 18.

[21] Then Peter came and said to him, 'Lord, if another member of the church sins against me, how often should I forgive? As many as seven times?' [22] Jesus said to him, 'Not seven times, but, I tell you, seventy-seven times. [23] For this reason the kingdom of heaven may be compared to a king who wished to settle accounts with his slaves. [24] When he began the reckoning, one who owed him ten thousand talents was brought to him; [25] and, as he could not pay, his lord ordered him to be sold, together with his wife and children and all his possessions, and payment to be made. [26] So the slave fell on his knees before him, saying, "Have patience with me, and I will pay you everything." [27] And out of pity for him, the lord of that slave released him and forgave him the debt. [28]

But that same slave, as he went out, came upon one of his fellow slaves who owed him a hundred denarii; and seizing him by the throat, he said, "Pay what you owe." [29] Then his fellow slave fell down and pleaded with him, "Have patience with me, and I will pay you." [30] But he refused; then he went and threw him into prison until he would pay the debt. [31] When his fellow slaves saw what had happened, they were greatly distressed, and they went and reported to their lord all that had taken place. [32] Then his lord summoned him and said to him, "You wicked slave! I forgave you all that debt because you pleaded with me. [33] Should you not have had mercy on your fellow slave, as I had mercy on you?" '

The offence of the ungrateful slave was his refusal to connect his own situation to that of a fellow victim's. This seems to fit one aspect of Jesus' doctrine of conditional forgiveness – only if we forgive others can we ourselves be forgiven – but a deeper reading may be possible. Is there some kind of universal awareness emerging here that by any calculus of revenge we would all deserve punishment for something, because we are all enmeshed in the web of collective guilt that history has spun round humanity? In real life, some are never punished, because they are never found out or because they are too powerful to be challenged; some are punished not for offences they did commit, but for those they did not commit; and some seem to be punished for no reason at all. The human situation, it is being suggested here, is so complex that it is impossible to apply a rational system of moral accountancy to it with any accuracy, so we should not even bother to try. Instead of laboriously working out the exact and proportionate revenge that is someone's due, we should refuse to get involved in the punishment process at all. Interestingly, the revenge system, though it appears to be the normal practice in most societies, does not seem to have been followed in every human community. The Blackfoot Indians of North America did not use such a system within their community, though they did impose the sanction of banishment on members who refused to comply with the group ethic. There was a sophisticated recognition among them that persistent offenders against the harmony of the community had, in effect, separated themselves from the life of the group, so banishment was an explicit recognition of the real situation, without resorting to any method of retributive punishment. What may be implicitly understood by communities that reject retributive punishment is the fact that once we stray into the web of revenge it wraps itself round us for ever, trapping us in the compulsions of vengeance and victimhood. The refusal to punish switches our attention from the actions themselves onto the agents who committed them, including the factors that influenced their conduct and which we should take account of when planning our response. There is an opposing moral tradition that dismisses this as a colossal mistake, because it holds that it is only acts we can accurately judge, never persons. The history of individuals is so complex that exactly judging their culpability is impossible; it is easier to decide whether their actions are objectively wrong and should be punished, because the law itself has to be vindicated for the sake of the community. This is a strictly logical position, but few of us would be prepared to say that moral acts can be completely separated from their human context, including the agent's level of awareness and intention.

In the Sermon on the Mount, Jesus cuts through the tangled complexity of the moral predicament and our search for the perfect proportionate response to human injustice: 'Don't even bother to try to work it out,' we can imagine him saying, 'don't start figuring out appropriate responses to injuries you have received. You'll just get sucked into a quagmire that will drown you. Move on, let it go, don't let resentment hijack your whole life, forgive, turn the other cheek. Don't let the imperative of revenge steal your future from you.' There is no sense here in which this is a cowardly or weak response to personal outrage. There is immense strength and dignity in it; and turning the other cheek is probably meant to be done with a sort of moral disdain for the assailant who is still trapped in the warped psychology of violence. 'You can play this dangerous game if you want', is the implication here, 'but my life and my right to direct it my way are too important for me to let you unsettle them with your games of vengeance. So, have a go at the other cheek, then get out of my life.'

To respond like this to the many ways the world can hurt and enrage us requires a high level of inner security and calm, and not everyone is endowed with that kind of strength. There's an entertaining example of it in the 1958 movie *The Big Country*. Gregory Peck is the modest sea captain from the East who goes West to marry Carroll Baker, the spoilt daughter of a million-aire rancher. Peck refuses to react to the hazing of the local cowboys, including the quick-tempered ranch-foreman, Charlton Heston, and infuriates his shallow fiancée, who wants him to respond the way she thinks a man of the Wild West ought to act. It is the delectable Jean Simmons, owner of a neighbouring ranch, who recognises that the Peck character is more interested in being true to his own code than in trying to impress the locals by conforming to theirs. In the end, of course, he wins the important fights as well as the better woman, but this is Hollywood, after all.

I want now to revisit something I said before. Since I believe it is important for us to avoid any suggestion of coercion in this sensitive area, I think it is better to talk about the complexities of forgiveness in the indicative rather than in the imperative mood. We do not have the right to order people to act in ways of which they are incapable, such as commanding them to forgive. The justice and revenge impulses are strong in us and seem to be intrinsic to our humanity. Even if we can identify many situations in history where these impulses have trapped people in unending spirals of revenge, we ought to acknowledge that a primitive kind of moral coherence is in operation there that we should not be too quick to condemn, particularly if we have never lived in similar situations. One of the difficulties with offering an appropriate moral judgment on the current war on terrorism is the recognition that, whether we thought it was the wisest thing to do in the long run, it was impossible for the USA not to offer some kind of response in kind to the original outrage against Manhattan and the Pentagon. When that sort of injury comes at you personally, your gut instinct is to respond in kind. This probably accounts for the surprising silence of the American left about the present conflict. There was a saying in the USA during the 1980s to the effect that a neo-conservative was a liberal who had been mugged on Boston Common the night before. That is why moralising at victims of crime and war is pointless and insulting. What is not pointless, however, is the kind of indicative approach that may help people to gain an understanding of the causes and possible consequences of their responses. Thinking before acting may enable them to take a step or two back from immediate retaliation and its ramifying repercussions into the future. It may be sexist to say so, but I wonder if women might not turn out to be an important part of international conflict resolution here. The revenge instinct seems to be hard-wired into the male of the human species. I know women can be fierce in the protection of their young, and there does seem to be something of an equal opportunities policy working in the area of violent crime at the moment, but the statistics of crime as well as the history of war demonstrate that both are fuelled to a great extent by blind testosterone. That is why managing male anger will always have to be a major factor in diminishing violence at both the personal and collective level.

Given the pressures and insecurities of male pride, refusing a fight can take enormous physical as well as moral courage. No one could accuse Jesus, Mahatma Ghandi or Martin Luther King of being physical cowards, yet they all espoused non-resistance as the best way of breaking the cycle of violence that plays on a permanent loop through human history. I am suggesting that, where the moral confidence exists to try it, the application of forgiveness to human conflict may break the chain of repetitive offending, though it is easier to follow this path in personal than in collective relationships.

Before exploring this further, I want to look at an aspect of the matter that goes beyond the sensible management of human impulses and brings us to an encounter with one of the mysteries of life, which is the experience of grace or gift. Strictly speaking, it is only here that we find pure or absolute forgiveness. All versions of conditional forgiveness, no matter how just, creative and releasing, are essentially tactical, designed to limit or manage the damage we do to one another. Pure forgiveness is not an instrumental good, a prudent management technique or a damage limitation exercise; it is an intrinsic good, an end in itself, a pure gift offered with no motive of return. The closest we come to it in human politics is the royal or presidential pardon that is offered to convicted criminals. Here no attempt is made to extenuate or explain away the crime: the criminal simply throws himself or herself on the mercy of the sovereign authority and the pardon comes, if it comes at all, as an unmerited gift. There is a radical reading of the parable of the prodigal son that sees within it this kind of unconditional love and forgiveness in action.

We left the delinquent son in the pigsty as he made up his mind to go back to his father, confess his sins and ask to be taken on as a hired hand. The story continues:

[20] So he set off and went to his father. But while he was still far off, his father saw him and was filled with compassion; he ran and put his arms around him and kissed him. [21] Then the son said to him, 'Father, I have sinned against heaven and before you; I am no longer worthy to be called your son.' [22] But the father said to his slaves, 'Quickly, bring out a robe – the best one – and put it on him; put a ring on his finger and sandals on his feet. [23] And get the fatted calf and kill it, and let us eat and celebrate; [24] for this son of mine was dead and is alive again; he was lost and is found!' And they began to celebrate. [25] Now his elder son was in the field; and when he came and approached the house, he heard music and dancing.

[26] He called one of the slaves and asked what was going on. [27] He replied, 'Your brother has come, and your father has killed the fatted calf, because he has got him back safe and sound.' [28] Then he became angry and refused to go in. His father came out and began to plead with him. [29] But he answered his father, 'Listen! For all these years I have been working like a slave for you, and I have never disobeyed your command; yet you have never given me even a young goat so that I might celebrate with my friends. [30] But when this son of yours came back, who has devoured your property with prostitutes, you killed the fatted calf for him!' [31] Then the father said to him, 'Son, you are always with me, and all that is mine is yours. [32] But we had to celebrate and rejoice, because this brother of yours was dead and has come to life; he was lost and has been found.'

In this reading of the parable, the central act is the running of the father to greet the returning sinner. His son had broken the strict patriarchal code of the community of which he had been a part. His request for his inheritance was an insult to his father and should have led to his banishment for rebellion. Instead, the broken-hearted father gives him what should legally have come to him only after his own death. Having abandoned the code that had been carefully designed to contain the anarchic and selfish human spirit, the son sinks even lower and finds himself living with pigs, animals of profound allegoric impurity in that culture. According to this reading of the parable, his coming to his senses was no act of repentance, but a character-istically opportunistic move that was designed to save his own skin. In deciding to try his luck at home, however, he will place himself in great danger, because he must run the gauntlet of the village elders, guardians of the moral code, before he can get to his father and make his bid for rescue. According to the code which he has already abandoned, he is no longer a part of the community he walked out of so contemptuously. If the elders see him enter the village, they will break an earthenware vessel over his head as a sign that he has shattered his covenant with the community and may henceforth be offered no succour, no food, no water, no shelter: he is already dead to them and they to him. The pining father sees him before anyone else *and runs to meet him*. This was in itself an extraordinary breach of the patriarchal code, which specified that the greater your dignity the more slowly you moved. Portentous deportment in our superiors is designed to awe or intimidate us, which is why pomposity is a common disguise of the inwardly fearful. The secure and fearless spirit has no need of protective camouflage and lives with an unselfconscious openness that responds spontaneously to the needs and overtures of others. The strong love of the waiting father has no interest in its own dignity or status. He rushes out to meet and embrace his disgraced child. It is this abandonment of code and conditionality that is the scandalous heart of the story. The son is clearly forgiven by the father before he can get a word out, and when he does produce his prepared speech there is a significant omission: 'Then the son said to him, "Father, I have sinned against heaven and before you; I am no longer worthy to be called your son," full stop. There is no opportunistic plea for a job on the farm. This reading of the parable suggests that the father's outpouring of love caused a true change in the son, so that we might say that the forgiveness that was unconditionally given actually caused the repentance that followed it, an exact reversal of the order that is followed in the usual system of conditional forgiveness. The parable ends inconclusively, because it closes with an act of petulant defiance of the father by the elder brother. Here, again, the father ignores the traditional code by *going out* to him to explain the nature of his heart's rejoicing at the return of his brother. Since the parable stops at this point, we do not know whether the older son also responded to the unconditional love of the father with a radical change of heart.

This is a story which, in George Steiner's words, 'casts fathomless light' on the human condition. It takes us completely away from the world that measures injuries and orders a carefully managed precision in our response to them. It simply tears up that script and substitutes an uncalculating mercy that makes no sense according to the conventional way of measuring these things, but which pours such sudden light upon our normal human motives that they are irradiated with the possibility of pure grace. There is a poem by Harry Smart called 'Praise' that captures something of the crazy mercy of such unconditional forgiveness:

> Praise be to God, who pities wankers
> and has mercy on miserable bastards.
> Praise be to God, who pours his blessing
> on reactionary warheads and racists.
>
> For he knows what he is doing; the healthy
> have no need of a doctor, the sinless
> have no need of forgiveness. But, you say,
> They do not deserve it. That is the point;

that is the point. When you try to wade
across the estuary at low tide, but misjudge
the distance, the currents, the soft ground
and are caught by the flood in deep schtuck,

then perhaps you will realise that God
is to be praised for delivering dickheads
from troubles they have made for themselves.
Praise be to God, who forgives sinners.

Let him who is without sin throw the first
headline. Let him who is without sin
build the gallows, prepare the noose,
say farewell to the convict with a kiss.[3]

We rarely see this kind of joyful mercy at work in
human history, but when we do it has enormous
redemptive value. It is one of the few things that
are able to break the circuit of evil within the heart
of the evil-doer; it is the kind of forgiveness that
Derrida must have been thinking about when he
wrote:

Yet despite all the confusions which reduce forgiveness to amnesty or to amnesia, to acquittal or pre-
scription, to the work of mourning or some political
therapy of reconciliation, in short to some historical

ecology, it must never be forgotten, nevertheless, that all of that refers to a certain idea of pure and unconditional forgiveness, without which this discourse would not have the least meaning . . . pure and unconditional forgiveness, in order to have its own meaning, must have no 'meaning', no finality, even no intelligibility. It is a madness of the impossible.[4]

It *is* a madness of the impossible, but when it occurs it can create a profound qualitative change in people and events. It is important to remember that it is not calculated to do this; it is not calculated to do anything; it is its own meaning, to use Derrida's language. Like pure poetry, which, according to W.H. Auden, makes nothing happen, radical forgiveness is its own meaning. In theological language, it is a miracle of pure unmerited grace, given out of uncalculating love. When it happens, if it ever happens, it casts not only light but silence all around, in which, one by one, the eager voices stop their clamour for revenge and fade away, the way the men who called for the stoning of the woman caught in adultery crept off the scene when Jesus invited the one without sin to cast the first stone. When we see this kind of imperturbable grace in action it leaves us in a state beyond explanation that is close to worship. Only this is absolute forgiveness, because only this forgives the unforgivable. There are some deeds that are so monstrous they will drive us mad if we do not forgive them, because no proportional reparation is possible, no just accounting, nothing that makes any sense. We cannot press a button to rewind history, to reverse the events of September 11, to get the planes back on the tarmac in Boston, to start that day again and let it follow its accustomed path. Those horrifying events are irreversible. The dead cannot return, the deed cannot be undone. Nor can the holocaust of the Jews nor the slave trade in Africans nor the genocide of the native American communities nor the ancient miseries of the poor in all places at all times. None of it can be undone, nor can it be appropriately avenged or made sense of. Only unconditional, impossible forgiveness can switch off the engine of madness and revenge and invite us, with infinite gentleness, to move on into the future. Until we can do that, we are exiled in the horror of the past, locked in the unspeakable nightmare. Sadly, unconditional forgiveness is beyond most of us, even though we believe it might be the very thing that could release us. It comes, when it comes at all, the way great genius suddenly visits us in extraordinary people.

One of the dismaying things about history is that there never seem to be many of these moral geniuses around. It is notoriously difficult to apply the politics of even conditional forgiveness to conflicts between groups or nations; it is almost impossible to apply unconditional forgiveness in these situations. The group mind is prone to the excitements of revenge and closed to the painstaking processes of forgiveness. Nevertheless, in situations of gross and enduring conflict between groups, the emergence of charismatic figures who bear in their own bodies the suffering of their people, yet are able to transcend the pain and lead them beyond it into the peace of forgiveness, is one of the most extraordinary spectacles that history affords. Such people become representative or archetypal figures who outgrow their own particular humanity and become universal figures. They are few enough at any time, but there seems to be a particular dearth of them today. Where is the great figure who can transcend the ancient conflicts in Northern Ireland or Israel/Palestine? There are good people at work in those places, of course, but no one has emerged as a fully representative, redemptive figure who is able to transcend the divisions and unite the opposite forces in the insane possibility of forgiveness. The only person who fully exemplifies this kind of impossibility today is Nelson Mandela. When Desmond Tutu spoke to me about Mandela the word he used to describe him was 'noble'.

I once stood outside the cell he had occupied on Robben Island and saw the thin mat on the cold floor on which he had slept for 18 years and was choked by the enormity of his graciousness. Those are the conditions that normally produce enraged avengers, whose actions we deplore, yet whose embittered logic we can understand. The enormity of forgiveness flowing from such conditions is impossible to understand. It is the insanity of grace. We hear it in the voice of the crucified forgiving those who are hammering in the nails. We hear it in the voice of the mother embracing in tears her daughter's killer and releasing in him the ability to own his own guilt for the first time. We hear it in the voice of Hosea drawing his adulterous wife back to him with the cords of love and tenderness. We call this kind of absolutely gratuitous conduct 'grace' or 'gift', because it comes upon us, when it comes at all, without condition. It is done for its own sake, out of the pure joy and love of doing it. Believers say it has its source in God, who pours out life without calculation from a pure excess of being. For those who do not believe in God or can find no meaning in this kind of language, the mystery remains that this prodigal universe sometimes redeems its own pain through extraordinary souls who, from somewhere beyond all possibility, forgive the unforgivable.

Of course, it is impossible to apply this kind of miraculous forgiveness in any systematic way to the grinding conflicts that disfigure our times. We can long and pray for the emergence of great figures who might help us to transcend our hatreds, but we all know the experience of passionate disagreement over how best to respond to the evils we constantly do to one another. Our instinct for justice, our strong sense that great injuries should be avenged and that atrocities should never go unpunished, is difficult to oppose. Nevertheless, the history of human vengeance is not one that contains much re-assurance for us. It suggests that, so complex are the conflicts that enmesh us and so unsubtle are the ways we respond to them, that violence goes on begetting further violence. If forgiveness, conditional or unconditional, is too difficult to apply in the heat of conflict between peoples and nations, then we might try to remember the healing power of mercy towards a vanquished enemy. In his famous speech on Conciliation with America in 1775 Edmund Burke said that 'Magnanimity in politics is not seldom the truest wisdom.' Magnanimity or political mercy is not as radical as forgiveness, but it is related to it and is easier to apply. Magnanimity is generosity in our dealings with those who oppose us, particularly those against whom we have successfully waged war.

Like its sister forgiveness, it can break the long chain of revenge. While it is almost as rare as forgiveness, it is often found in great leaders, including great warriors. Where it is present after a great conflict it can check the infection of future violence. Its absence after an overwhelming victory can allow the seeds of hatred to grow towards a terrible harvest. In January 1919, W.B. Yeats wrote one of his most prophetic poems, 'The Second Coming':

> Turning and turning in the widening gyre
> The falcon cannot hear the falconer;
> Things fall apart; the centre cannot hold;
> Mere anarchy is loosed upon the world . . .
>
> And what rough beast, its hour come round at last,
> Slouches towards Bethlehem to be born?[5]

The most tragic example of the failure of a great nation to practise magnanimity or political forgiveness towards its defeated enemy, and thereby release the rough beast of history, is found in William Manchester's biography of Winston Churchill. He quotes Churchill's own words the day the Great War ended:

> It was a few minutes before the eleventh hour of the eleventh day of the eleventh month. I stood at the

window of my room looking up Northumberland Avenue to Trafalgar Square, waiting for Big Ben to tell that the War was over.

Manchester says that, when Big Ben struck, Churchill could hear the baying of the crowds, but felt no jubilation. Since 1914 Britain had suffered 908,371 dead, 2,090,212 wounded, and 191,652 missing. Victory had been 'bought so dear as to be indistinguishable from defeat'. Churchill's wife proposed that they go to Downing Street and congratulate Lloyd George, the Prime Minister. Those already present when Churchill arrived were discussing the advantage of calling a general election. Churchill interrupted to point out that the 'fallen foe' was close to starvation. He proposed rushing 'a dozen great ships crammed with provisions' to Hamburg, but his proposal was coldly rejected. Manchester tells us that, while Churchill's suggestion was being rebuffed by his unforgiving colleagues, a twice-decorated German non-commissioned despatch runner, who had been temporarily blinded during a heavy gas attack on the night of October 13, sat in a Pomeranian military hospital and learnt of Germany's plight from a sobbing pastor. Six years later the soldier set down a description of his reaction to the event:

I knew that all was lost. Only fools, liars and criminals could hope for mercy from the enemy. In these nights hatred grew in me, hatred for those responsible for this deed . . . The more I tried to achieve clarity on the monstrous events in this hour, the more the shame of indignation and disgrace burned my brow. What was all the pain in my eyes compared to this misery? In the days that followed, my own fate became known to me . . . I resolved to go into politics.[6]

The soldier's name was Adolf Hitler.

Notes

Chapter 1

1. John D. Caputo, *On Religion*, Routledge, London and New York, 2001, pp.138–139.
2. Ibid., pp.112–113.
3. Richard Rorty, *Philosophy and Social Hope*, Penguin, London, 1999, pp.201 and 209.
4. Jacques Derrida, *On Cosmopolitanism and Forgiveness*, Routledge, London and New York, 2001, pp.30–31.
5. Ibid., pp.32–33.

Chapter 2

1. Harry Golden, *Only in America*, Permabooks, New York, 1959, p.1.
2. Friedrich Nietzsche, *The Will to Power*, Vintage, New York, 1968, p.12.
3. Martin Amis, *Experience*, Vintage, London, 2001, p.189, where a version of the encounter is described.
4. Edwin Morgan, *Collected Poems*, Carcanet Press, Manchester, 1996, p.170.
5. Friedrich Nietzsche, *Beyond Good and Evil*, part 9, section 257, *Basic*

[93]

Writings of Nietzsche, The Modern Library, New York, 1992, pp. 391–392.

6. Sigmund Freud, *Civilization, Society and Religion*, Penguin, London, 1991, p.194.

7. Julia Kristeva, *Hannah Arendt*, Columbia University Press, New York, 2001, p.206.

8. Friedrich Nietzsche, *On the Genealogy of Morals*, First Essay, section 10, Oxford University Press, Oxford, 1996.

9. Friedrich Nietzsche, *Untimely Meditations*, Cambridge University Press, Cambridge, 1997, p.62.

10. Hannah Arendt, *The Portable Hannah Arendt*, Penguin, London, 2000, pp.180–181.

11. Kristeva, *Hannah Arendt*, p.232.

Chapter 3

1. Rebecca West, alias 'Conway Power', epigraph to, *The Birds Fall Down*, Virago, London, 1986.

2. Norman MacCaig, *Selected Poems*, Chatto and Windus, London, 1997, p.112.

3. Albert Camus, *The Outsider*, Penguin, London, 1981, pp.119, 120.

4. Gerard Manley Hopkins, *Poems*, Oxford University Press, London, 1948, p.110.

5. T.S.Eliot, *The Complete Poems and Plays*, Harcourt, Brace and Company, New York, 1952, p.141.

6. Derrida, *Cosmopolitanism and Forgiveness*, p.43.

Chapter 4

1. Adam Phillips, *The Beast in the Nursery*, London, 1998, p.98.

2. George Steiner, *Errata*, Phoenix, London, 1997, pp.57–60.

3. Harry Smart, *Fools Pardon*, Faber and Faber, London.

4. Derrida, *Cosmopolitanism and Forgiveness*, p.45.
5. W.B. Yeats, *The Poems*, Everyman, London, 1998, p.235.
6. William Manchester, *The Last Lion: Winston Spencer Churchill, Visions of Glory 1874–1932*, Little, Brown and Company, Boston, 1983, pp.650–651.

Bibliography

Amis, Martin, *Experience*, Vintage, London, 2001

Arendt, Hannah, *The Portable Hannah Arendt*, Penguin, London, 2000

Camus, Albert, *The Outsider*, Penguin, London, 1981

Caputo, John D., *On Religion*, Routledge, London and New York, 2001

Derrida, Jacques, *On Cosmopolitanism and Forgiveness*, Routledge, London and New York, 2001

Eliot, T.S., *The Complete Poems and Plays*, Harcourt, Brace and Company, New York, 1952

Freud, Sigmund, *Civilization, Society and Religion*, Penguin, London, 1991

Golden, Harry, *Only in America*, Permabooks, New York, 1959

Hopkins, Gerard Manley, *Poems*, Oxford University Press, London, 1948

Kristeva, Julia, *Hannah Arendt*, Columbia University Press, New York, 2001

MacCaig, Norman, *Selected Poems*, Chatto and Windus, London, 1997

Manchester, William, *The Last Lion: Winston Spencer Churchill, Visions of Glory 1874–1932*, Little, Brown and Company, Boston, 1983

Morgan, Edwin, *Collected Poems*, Carcanet Press, Manchester, 1996

Nietzsche, Friedrich, *The Will to Power*, Vintage, New York, 1968

Nietzsche, Friedrich, *Beyond Good and Evil, Basic Writings of Nietzsche*, The Modern Library, New York, 1992

Nietzsche, Friedrich, *On the Genealogy of Morals*, Oxford University Press, Oxford, 1996

Nietzsche, Friedrich, *Untimely Meditations*, Cambridge University Press, Cambridge, 1997

Waltham Forest Libraries and Information

Customer name: Richards, Charell (Miss)
Customer ID: *****214811

Items that you have borrowed

Title: Better conversations: achieving success at work & in life, one conversation at a time
ID: 90400_____764
Due: 19 March 2024

Total items: 1
Account ___ ___
27/02/20__ __:__
Borrowed 1
Overdue 0
Hold requests: 0
Ready for collection: 0

Thank you for using ___ ___ service
Need to renew ___ ___
www.londonlibrar___ ___ ___
dial 020 8496 ____
You will need your ___ ___ ___ please
speak to a member ___

Phillips, Adam, *The Beast in the Nursery*, Faber and Faber, London, 1998
Rorty, Richard, *Philosophy and Social Hope*, Penguin, London, 1999
Smart, Harry, *Fools Pardon*, Faber and Faber, London, 1995
George Steiner, *Errata*, Phoenix, London, 1997
West, Rebecca [alias Power, Conway], *The Birds Fall Down*, Virago, London, 1986
Yeats, W.B., *The Poems*, Everyman, London, 1998

Permissions Credits

Extracts from *On Cosmopolitanism and Forgiveness*, Jacques Derrida, Routledge, London and New York, 2001 are reproduced by permission of Taylor & Francis Books Ltd.

The extract from 'Little Gidding' by T.S. Eliot is taken from *The Complete Poems and Plays*, Harcourt Brace and Company, New York, 1952. Permission sought.

'Praise of a Collie' from *Collected Poems* by Norman MacCaig published by Chatto & Windus. Used by permission of The Random House Group Limited.

'In the Snackbar' is taken from *Collected Poems*, Edwin Morgan, Carcanet Press, Manchester, 1996. Reproduced by permission.

'Praise' is taken from *Fools Pardon* by Harry Smart, Faber and Faber Ltd, London, 1995. Reproduced by permission.

The poem by Conway Power (a pseudonym of Rebecca West) is reproduced from *The Birds Fall Down* by Rebecca West (Copyright © Rebecca West 1966) by permission of PFD on behalf of the Estate of Rebecca West.

Extract from 'The Second Coming' is taken from *The Poems*, W. B. Yeats, Everyman, London, 1998. Reproduced by permission of A. P. Watt Ltd on behalf of Michael B. Yeats (in the UK). Reprinted with the permission of Scribner, a division of Simon & Schuster, Inc., from *The Collected Works of W. B. Yeats: Volume 1, The Poems*, revised, edited by Richard J. Finneran. Copyright © 1924 by The MacMillan Company; copyright renewed 1952 by Bertha Georgie Yeats (in the US).